Famous Landmarks

HEINLE
CENGAGE Learning

Y|S|G
A YBM COMPANY
Young & Son
Global, Inc.

What are some famous places in your country?

Buckingham Palace,
London, England

Contents

Vocabulary

landmarks

famous

statue

Namdaemun, Seoul, South Korea

wall

tomb

tower

Landmarks on a Map

What are landmarks?
Landmarks are famous places.
People come from all over the world
to visit these landmarks.

Franc
Paris

U.S.A.
New York ●

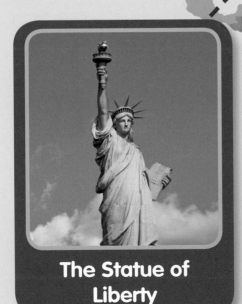
The Statue of Liberty

The Great Sphinx of Giza

The Eiffel Tower

N
W   E
S

China
Beijing

Egypt
Giza

India
Agra

The Taj Mahal

The Great Wall of China

The Statue of Liberty holds a torch and a book.

The Statue of Liberty

The Statue of Liberty is in New York City, the United States of America. It was a gift from France to America in 1886. The French built the statue to show their friendship.

Today, it is a symbol of America's freedom.

building the statue's arm

Millions of people visit the Great Wall of China every year.

The Great Wall of China

The Great Wall of China stretches across the north of China.
Over 2,000 years ago, Emperor Qin started building the wall to protect the country. Over the years, later emperors made the wall bigger and longer.
Now, it is the longest wall in the world.

CHINA

BEIJING

The Great Wall of China
is over 8,800 kilometers long.

The Taj Mahal

The Taj Mahal is in Agra, India, and is over 350 years old. It is a tomb for the wife of the emperor Shah Jahan. He was very sad when she died and built the Taj Mahal to remember her.

Shah Jahan and his wife

The Eiffel Tower

The Eiffel Tower is in Paris, France.

Gustave Eiffel built it in 1889 and it was the tallest building in the world for over 40 years. Today, people still go up the tower to see all of Paris.

people under the Eiffel Tower in 1889

The Great Sphinx of Giza

The Great Sphinx of Giza is in Egypt. It is one of the largest and oldest statues in the world. People still do not know when the Sphinx was built or who built it. Why it was built is also a mystery.

The Great Sphinx of Giza has a human head and a lion's body.

Summary

Where are these landmarks?

Use a Compass Rose

A **compass rose** shows directions on a map. The four main directions are north, south, east, and west.

The Eiffel Tower

North
N
West W — E East
S
South

France
Paris

China
Beijing

U.S.A.
New York

Egypt
Giza

India
Agra

The Statue of Liberty

The Great Sphinx of Giza

The Taj Mahal

The Great Wall of China

1. Is the Eiffel Tower north or south of the Great Sphinx of Giza?

2. Which landmark is west of the Eiffel Tower?

3. Put your finger on the Statue of Liberty. Now move your finger to the Great Wall of China. In which direction did you move?

Glossary

emperor
A man who rules an empire or a group of countries

freedom
Being able to do what you want

mystery
Something that is difficult or impossible to understand or explain

protect
To keep someone or something safe from harm, injury, or damage

symbol
A sign, shape, or object used to represent or mean something

visit
To go to a place for a short period of time

Index